Players & the Game
Around the World

Mason Crest
450 Parkway Drive, Suite D
Broomall, PA 19008
www.masoncrest.com

Printed and bound in the United States of America.

First printing
9 8 7 6 5 4 3 2 1

Series ISBN: 978-1-4222-3101-2
ISBN: 978-1-4222-3110-4
ebook ISBN: 978-1-4222-8800-9

Cataloging-in-Publication Data on file with the Library of Congress.

Contents

KEY ICONS TO LOOK FOR:

Text-Dependent Questions: These questions send the reader back to the text for more careful attention to the evidence presented there.

Words to Understand: These words with their easy-to-understand definitions will increase the reader's understanding of the text, while building vocabulary skills.

Series Glossary of Key Terms: This back-of-the book glossary contains terminology used throughout this series. Words found here increase the reader's ability to read and comprehend higher-level books and articles in this field.

Research Projects: Readers are pointed toward areas of further inquiry connected to each chapter. Suggestions are provided for projects that encourage deeper research and analysis.

Sidebars: This boxed material within the main text allows readers to build knowledge, gain insights, explore possibilities, and broaden their perspectives by weaving together additional information to provide realistic and holistic perspectives.

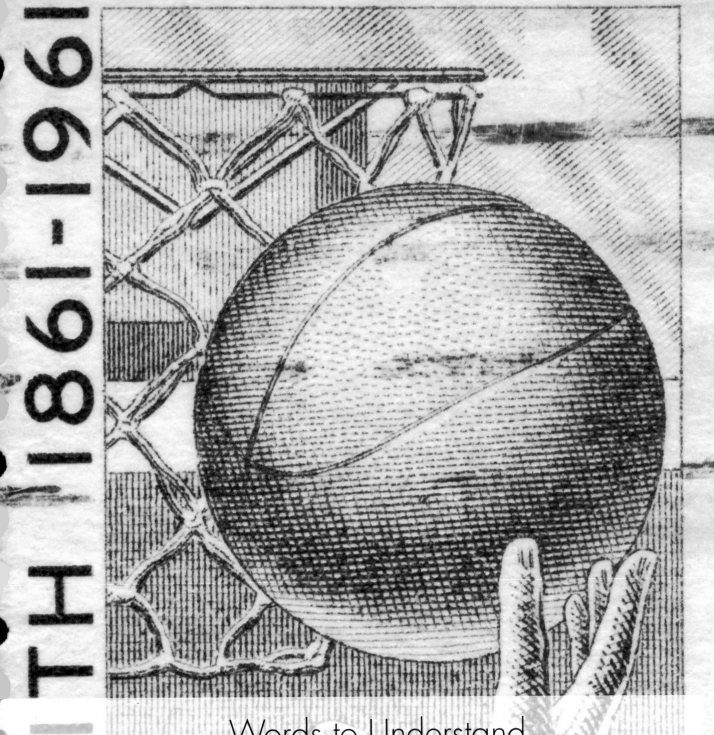

Words to Understand

philosophy: A person's or group's basic beliefs and ideas.

improvise: Perform spontaneously and on the spur of the moment, without following any set rules.

prejudice: Unfairly judging someone you don't know.

discrimination: Unfairly treating people in different ways based on sex, race, etc.

segregated: Separated by race, gender, or religion.

A Game That Bridged Differences

Basketball started out with peach baskets and ladders. Today, the sport has grown into a major industry and way of life for millions of people all around the world. However, the basics remain: you still have to throw a ball through a hoop! And the game of basketball is still a force to bridge differences between all sorts of different people.

THE BIRTH OF BASKETBALL

During December of 1891, a Canadian physical educator named James Naismith wanted a sport his students could play during the long winters.

Naismith had started out thinking he would be a minister, because he wanted to help others. However, one day while he was watching a football game, he realized the power sports have to shape people. He understood, he said, that "there might be other ways of doing good besides preaching."

A sculpture of James Naismith honors his contribution to the world of basketball.

PLAYERS & THE GAME AROUND THE WORLD

Make Connections

Several changes have been made since the early days of basketball. Naismith's players wore wool jerseys with long sleeves and long pants, while today, players wear light jerseys so they can move more easily, with matching colors and individualized numbers so people can recognize them better. Originally, shots from the field had to be two-handed. If a player fouled, then anyone on the opposing team could shoot the free throw. Teams also could have any number of players (in 1892, Cornell University had fifty players on each side) before the number was fixed at five. Despite Naismith's goals for basketball, many of the early games were a lot rougher than basketball is today, often ending in fights and arguments. Wire cages were put up around the court to protect the audiences, and to prevent the audience from throwing bottles and other garbage onto the court. Some referees even carried guns as a means of controlling the games!

Naismith got a job with the YMCA, which had the same ideas he did about sports. The YMCA's **philosophy** was that sports would not only strengthen the bodies of urban kids, but that it would also help them to become better people. Naismith got a job at the YMCA in Springfield, Massachusetts, ready to put his ideas into practice.

But he ran into problems. The players at the YMCA—young men in their late teens and early twenties—were a rough bunch. They spent a lot of their time at the Y fighting with each other. In the YMCA gymnasium, Naismith tried to channel the men's restlessness through indoor soccer and lacrosse. However, these sports weren't good for playing inside four walls. The games broke down into fights. Players ended up injured, and the walls and floors were damaged.

So Naismith decided to invent his own sport. He wanted no roughhousing in his gym—but he did want a challenging sport that would take skill. He also wanted a game that would allow players to **improvise**. The young men who came to the Y had too many rules in their lives as it was; they needed a place where they could be free to solve their own problems, where their individual intelligence and skill would have room to grow.

So Naismith jotted down some simple rules on a sheet of paper, and then he nailed two peach baskets high on the walls of the gym. The first game was played with a soccer ball and nine students on each team (because Naismith had eighteen students). A janitor was convinced to climb a ladder to retrieve the ball each time someone made a basket. Fortunately for the janitor, the first game ended with a score of 1–0.

By the time Naismith and his students had played the new game a few times, they

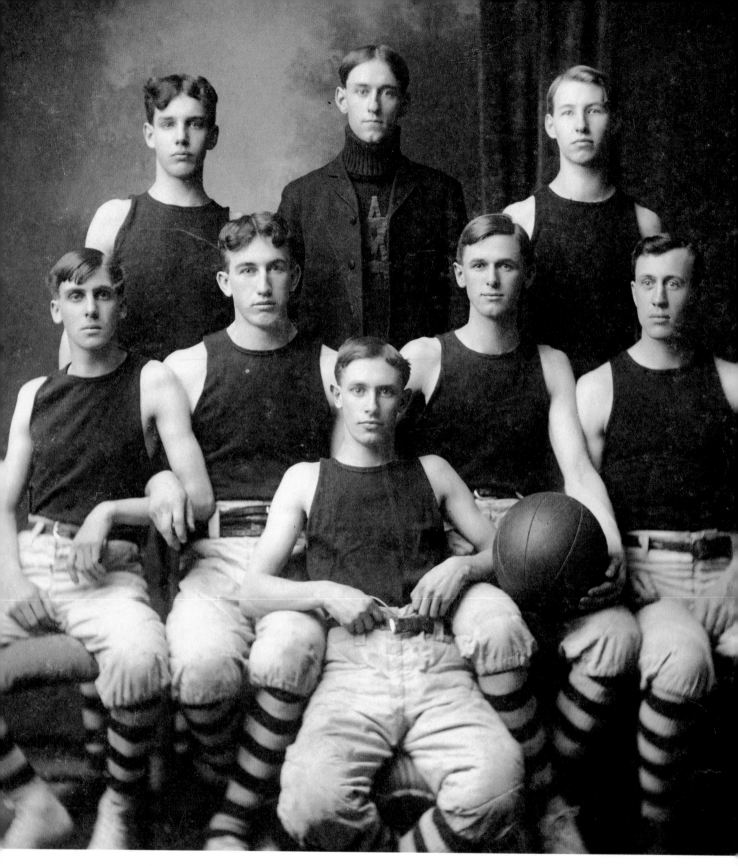

One of the early basketball teams played for Michigan State University.

Make Connections

When women first started playing basketball back in the nineteenth century, they were expected to wear floor-length dresses, petticoats, and slippers. Greater freedom came in 1896 when bloomers were introduced to women at Sophie Newcomb College in New Orleans. However, as women's basketball started to gain popularity, the nation was outraged to see well-bred women pulling hair, yelling, and shrieking. Parents, doctors, and physical education teachers were afraid to encourage girls to play in the sport. Women who did participate were encouraged to wear makeup for the games to help them look more dignified. Some teams required that their players wear wigs! However, gradually, women's basketball became more widely accepted, and by 2002, the Women's National Basketball Association (WNBA) drew in over two million viewers.

decided to remove the bottoms of the baskets; now the janitor could put away his ladder. Eventually, peach baskets were exchanged for wires, and a backboard was added.

The young men loved the game. They stopped fighting with each other and started working together to improve their skills. Basketball gave them something in common, something they all loved. Playing was a lot more fun than fighting.

Before long, the sport caught on in other YMCAs across the United States. By 1897, teams of five players were standard. And the game kept spreading. Basketball was on its way.

AN ALL-AMERICAN SPORT

At first, basketball was most popular as a game city kids could play indoors without a lot of expensive equipment. During the last part of the nineteenth century and the first part of the twentieth century, immigrants flooded American cities. Sports—especially basketball—were a way for these immigrants' children to fit in with other Americans.

America's rural areas had baseball—but the cities had basketball. All sorts of urban organizations had basketball teams, from labor unions to department stores, from factories to churches and synagogues. Basketball thrived in America's busy cities. It was a way for people from very different ethnic backgrounds to come together.

But one group of Americans was left out: black Americans. One man, Edwin Bancroft Henderson, wanted to change that. Henderson had grown up in Washington, D.C., playing baseball with his friends in the streets. In high school, he was a football star. Once he

Text-Dependent Questions

1. Who was the inventor of basketball and why did he want to create a new game?
2. What was the janitor's job in the first basketball games?
3. Using the first sidebar, list four ways that basketball has changed since it was first invented.
4. Explain what Edwin Henderson did for basketball.
5. This chapter states that basketball has the power to unite different types of people. Give two examples of this from the chapter.

graduated, he went on to a two-year college that prepared African Americans to teach in Washington, D.C.'s black schools, and from there he went to a physical training program at Harvard University. It was at Harvard, in 1904, that Henderson first encountered basketball.

Henderson loved the game. At the same time, he began to realize something: the playing field was the one place at that time where blacks and whites could be equal, bound by the exact same rules. For Henderson, like for Naismith, sports were more than simply exercise or fun—they were a way to make the world a better place. If blacks could do well at basketball, Henderson reasoned, basketball could cross the terrible walls of *prejudice* and *discrimination*. It would prove that white supremacy was a lie.

Henderson came home from Harvard and took a job as a gym teacher in one of D.C.'s *segregated* schools. He started a black sports league, where he introduced his students to basketball. He also played the game himself.

Henderson was a great basketball player, and so were his students. But no matter how good black players were, the white community didn't know about them, because only white players were on the city's organized leagues. So one night in 1907, Henderson and a friend walked into a YMCA game. They hoped that the YMCA, with its focus on Christian brotherhood, might be able to accept them.

Instead, Henderson and his friend were thrown out and told to never return. Henderson realized he would have to form all-black leagues instead. In 1908, he did just that. The leagues played at night in front of crowds who danced to live music after the games.

Black Americans loved the new sport. But black basketball and white basketball were two separate things. Henderson was not giving up, though. For the next few decades he not only played and coached basketball—he also wrote books, magazine articles, and letters to newspapers, explaining why blacks should be able to participate in basketball in particular and sports in general.

Make Connections

In 2013, Henderson's achievements in the world of basketball were officially recognized when he was elected into the Basketball Hall of Fame. Edwin Henderson did even more with his life than fight for black basketball, though. He also influenced many young people in the black community who would go on to shine in other ways. Two of these were Duke Ellington, the great composer and bandleader, and Charles Drew, a surgeon and medical researcher, each of whom proved in their own way that black Americans were just as talented and intelligent as whites. Henderson and his wife were also active in the civil rights movement, fighting tirelessly against discrimination in housing and education.

Finally, thanks in part to Henderson's hard work, the basketball world opened up to black players. By 1915, blacks were playing alongside whites on high school and college basketball teams.

But it wasn't as easy to break the racial barriers in professional basketball. Basketball still had a long way to go.

Research Project

Find out more about the history of women's basketball. Use the Internet and the library to find the answers to these questions:

• What did women's uniforms look like? Find pictures to illustrate your answer.
• When and how did women players' uniforms change?
• What woman was responsible for getting women's basketball started?
• What were some of the specific complaints made about women playing basketball?
• What role did basketball play in the women's rights movement?
• What is women's basketball like today?

Put your answers together into a report.

Words to Understand

boycott: Refuse to buy something or go somewhere out of protest.
minorities: Groups of people who are regularly discriminated against.
integrated: Allowing all groups of people to participate and not be separated out or left out.

How Basketball Spread Around the World

After Naismith's invention of the game, basketball not only spread across America; it also spread across the oceans, while at the same time it traveled south, down into Central and South America. Wherever it went, it continued to build bridges. Basketball wasn't just a fun, exciting game; it was something that united people around the world.

The YMCA, the organization James Naismith worked for, was international; there were Ys all over the world, and YMCA workers carried the new game to all the countries where their organization was active. Basketball spread first to Naismith's home country, Canada. Then YMCA members from England brought the game home with them after a visit to Canada in 1892. Next, thanks again to YMCA members, the first basketball game was played in France in 1893. The following year, again thanks to the YMCA, basketball was played for the first time in China, India, Japan, and Iran. In 1909, YMCA basketball players traveled to St. Petersburg, Russia, for the very first international match.

This game between a French team and a U.S. team was played in 1919. The French still had a lot to learn, though: the score was 93 to 8, in favor of the American team.

When the United States entered World War I in 1917, American soldiers brought basketball with them wherever they went, and it continued to spread. The first South American basketball championship was played in 1930. It wasn't only league basketball that was taking off, though; kids and adults were playing pick-up games in streets and parks and gyms all around the world.

THE FORMATION OF FIBA

In 1932, the first international basketball organization was created to coordinate tournaments and teams. Basketball leagues from Argentina, Czechoslovakia, Greece, Italy, Latvia, Portugal, Romania, and Switzerland got together in Geneva, Switzerland, and together they formed the International Basketball Federation. In French, the organization was called *Fédération internationale de basket-ball amateur*, which was shortened to FIBA.

FIBA was so successful that when it came time for the Olympic Games in 1936, the International Olympic Committee added basketball as a medal sport. Around the world, the best basketball teams started getting their players ready to compete with the rest of the world.

Make Connections

At the 1936 Olympics, FIBA decided to name James Naismith as its Honorary President.

BASKETBALL TAKES A STAND AT THE OLYMPICS

In the United States that year, the Blackbirds of Long Island University had just had a fantastic season with 33 straight wins and an average victory margin of 23 points. Most Americans were sure that the Blackbirds would be the team representing America at the Olympic Games in Berlin, Germany.

In the early years of basketball, Native Americans were already playing the game. This girls' team played for a school in South Dakota.

During the Olympics, Adolph Hitler tried to hide the extent of Nazi persecution of Jews. Here, he salutes at the opening ceremonies.

Instead, the Blackbirds decided to walk away from the Olympics.

After World War I, Germany lay in ruins. In 1931, the Olympic Committee decided to give Germany the honor of hosting the Summer Olympics as a symbol that the war was truly over, and the world community was once more united. Then, in 1933, the Nazi political party rose to power in Germany. Adolph Hitler was now Germany's leader.

The Nazis believed that a certain kind of white people were superior to all other groups of people. They wanted to get rid of Jews, Gypsies, homosexuals, and pretty much anyone else who was different or disagreed with them. No Jews were allowed to play on Germany's sports teams, and Germany would be sending no Jewish athletes to the Olympics.

People around the world weren't happy about what Hitler was doing in Germany, but they didn't yet realize just how bad things were—nor did they know how truly terrible things would soon become. Some people pushed hard for their countries to **boycott** the Berlin Olympics, as a way of showing that the world would not stand by and accept what the Nazis were doing. In the end, though, the world decided to go ahead with the Olympics. They hoped it would be a way to build peace.

But the Blackbirds disagreed. Every single member of the team voted to boycott the Olympics. Odds were good that they would have been Olympic winners, an enormous honor and achievement for any athlete. But they gave up their chance at the Olympic gold. They stayed true to James Naismith's original goal for basketball as a game that does good in the world.

Instead, the United States sent to the Olympics a team sponsored by Universal Pictures (the movie production company). The German organizers decided to hold the basketball games on an outdoor court made of clay and sand. The gold medal game was played in heavy rain that turned the court to a sea of mud. The United States won, while Canada came in second, but not very many points were scored: the score was only 19 to 8.

Today, the Harlem Globetrotters are an exhibition basketball team that combines athleticism, theater, and comedy. Their antics are meant to make people laugh, but they also take a lot of skill.

During World War II, the U.S. government "relocated" many Japanese Americans to internment camps; because the United States was also at war with Japan, many Americans did not trust Americans with Japanese ancestry. Basketball, the all-American sport, was a part of camp life. This game between girls' teams was played in a relocation center in Wyoming in 1944.

WORLD WAR II

Eventually, the world could no longer turn a blind eye to Hitler and the Nazis. War broke out in 1939, and the United States got involved in 1941. With so many men off at war, many colleges had to drop their basketball games. Professional basketball teams threatened to do the same.

But many Americans didn't want to give up what had become their favorite sport. President Franklin Delano Roosevelt decided that professional basketball should continue through the war. A good game, he said, would provide much needed relief to a war-weary country.

With so many men off to war, women and **minorities** had new opportunities to shine on the basketball court. All-black teams now took on white teams. One of the big teams to come out of this era was the Harlem Globetrotters. In those days, they were a serious team that won the World Basketball Tournament in 1941, but even then, audiences enjoyed the entertainment the Globetrotters provided while they played.

Meanwhile, troops fighting around the world enjoyed a game of basketball whenever they had a chance. The soldiers brought basketball with them everywhere they went, and the game continued to spread.

INTEGRATING BASKETBALL

After the war, professional basketball took off again. White players were once more at the forefront of the sport. In 1949, the National Basketball Association (NBA) was born when two leagues, the National Basketball League and the Basketball Association of America, merged. Basketball kept growing, as more and more people fell in love with this fast-paced game. But the first black NBA player wasn't until 1950. His name was Earl Lloyd.

Joining an all-white team was a scary step for Earl Lloyd, but his teammates—most of whom had already played on **integrated** college teams—welcomed him. Some fans, however, weren't as kind. As the announcer read the lineup on Lloyd's first night, a white

Text-Dependent Questions

1. What is FIBA and when did it begin?
2. How did World War I and World War II contribute to the growth of basketball?
3. Why did the Blackbirds refuse to play at the Olympics, even though they probably would have brought home the gold?
4. Explain how basketball helped to break down racial barriers in the United States.

Wilt Chamberlain started out in the 1950s playing for the Harlem Globetrotters. He was one of the players who proved how amazing black players could be on the basketball court.

man in the front row shouted, "Do you think this n—— can play any basketball?" Lloyd's mother happened to be sitting right behind the man; she leaned forward and told him not to worry. "The n——," she said, "can play."

CHANGING THE WORLD

During these years, basketball was doing its part to change the world. It helped to bridge the racial barriers between Americans—and it was also uniting people around the world. FIBA held the first World Championship in 1950, followed by a World Championship for Women in 1953. In the years that followed, both events were held every four years.

Meanwhile, without black Americans, basketball would not have risen to the heights it has. Black players like Wilt Chamberlain, Magic Johnson, Scottie Pippin, and Karl Malone were as popular with white basketball fans as they were with black fans. Black Americans had done exactly what Edwin Henderson had hoped—and then some! They more than proved to the world that African Americans excelled on the basketball court. In fact, by 2014, the NBA was more than three-quarters black.

Basketball had become a global sport played by people of all skin colors, all around the world.

Words to Understand

missionaries: People who go to other parts of the world to persuade the people who live there to convert to Christianity.

work ethic: The idea that hard work is good or valuable for its own sake.

perks: Benefits.

solidarity: Unity or agreement.

camaraderie: Trust and friendship between people who spend a lot of time together.

economic: Having to do with business and money.

GLOBAL BASKETBALL

Basketball today touches every nation in the world. Its growth has been amazing. Only forty-nine years after James Naismith invented the game, players were getting paid to be basketball pros. By the time Naismith died in 1939, his original rules for the game had been translated into fifty different languages.

The YMCA and the armed forces had helped to spread the game. So had **missionaries** to remote areas of the world, who brought the game with them, along with the Christian faith. The NBA, however, was the organization that did the most to bring the game to other cultures around the world, starting in the 1980s.

In 1983, the first NBA games were televised in Italy. It was the first time viewers outside the United States were able to see the games. Soon, though, basketball was in people's homes everywhere there was television. Now, each region of the world was exposed to basketball at a far wider level than every before.

A reproduction of an ancient drawing shows the "basketball game," played in Mexico about 1500 years ago.

BASKETBALL IN LATIN AMERICA

Today, from Mexico to Chile, kids are playing basketball in the streets and on dusty outdoor courts. At the professional level, though, the game has to compete with this region's number-one sport: *futból* (soccer).

Soccer's influence on basketball is very obvious in Latin America's informal street games. Players raised on soccer tend to pass more than dribble. In some countries, however, like Argentina and Brazil, where basketball has been around longer and is more established, coaches take advantage of this tendency to build players who have very strong teamwork and footwork skills.

Make Connections

Some people like to say that the first basketball games were played long, long ago in Mexico and Central America. This ancient game did use balls that were thrown through hoops—but it was a very different game from the one that's played today. The game was played in a brick trench, with hoops fastened to the walls of the trench, placed at various heights and distances apart. The players did not dribble the ball; instead, they tossed it back and forth until one of them could toss the ball through a hoop. The balls were made of solid rubber and weighed as much as 9 pounds (4 kg); according to some stories, human heads were sometimes used instead of balls. Games could last for hours, and winning was literally a matter of life and death: the losing team was killed. The game had serious religious and political meanings, and was probably done as part of a ritual. However, children and women also played it just for fun (and no one died in these games).

Basketball fans started to really take notice of Latino basketball players in 2002, when Manu Ginobili from Argentina joined the San Antonio Spurs—and then went on to score double digits in points per game throughout 2003. Other Latin American players were proving their worth as well, including the Brazilian Nené and another Argentinean, Luis Scola.

Once Latino players got started in the NBA, they didn't stop. Puerto Rico's Rafael "Piculin" Ortiz is one of the most famous Latino players. He lead the Puerto Rican National team at the 2004 Olympic Games in Athens—where they stunned the United States team by beating them 92 to 73 at their first game.

Since the 1992 Olympics, America's Dream Team had been the shining stars of international basketball. But at the 2004 Olympics, both Puerto Rico and Argentina beat the U.S. team. The Puerto Rican and Argentinean teams proved to the world that Latino players could bring their own style of play to the game—and win. Latinos are serious basketball players.

When James Naismith first imagined the game, he wanted something where players could improvise and show their individual strengths. Latino players are doing just that. Today's NBA benefits from the strengths Latino players bring from their home cultures. For example, Eduardo Najera's hustle on the court was modeled on the energetic **work ethic** he learned growing up in Mexico. Felipe Lopez and Francisco Garcia's passion and fire on the court were qualities they learned in their homeland, the Dominican Republic. Latino players all bring their own unique styles of play. They are helping to build basketball into a truly global game.

Nenê, a Brazilian player, scores in a 2011 game between the Washington Wizards and the Denver Nuggets.

The first Latino player in the NBA was Alfred "Butch" Lee from Puerto Rico, who was drafted in 1978 by the Atlanta Hawks. He scored close to 10 points per game his rookie year, but he played only a few more seasons due to a serious injury. Before he retired, though, he collected a championship ring with Magic Johnson and the Lakers. Lee returned to his homeland and became one of the most respected head coaches in the National Superior Basketball League.

Other Latin American players who reached the NBA include Puerto Rican Ramon Rivas and Horacio Llamas, who in 1996 became the first Mexican in the NBA.

In a region of the world where poverty is common, basketball inspires people. They look up to NBA players as examples of people who have achieved something amazing against the odds.

BASKETBALL IN AFRICA

The same thing is happening across Africa. Soccer may still be the number-one sport in most of Africa, but basketball is growing fast. The NBA believes the continent will provide future stars, as well as millions of new fans.

The NBA has launched a program called "Basketball without Borders." It is working hard to reach out to young people in Africa, as well as other places of the world. The NBA also believes that if basketball games are televised across Africa, more players will be drafted from Africa. In 2013, the NBA signed a deal with a South African broadcast company to televise the 2013–14 season in forty-seven sub-Saharan territories.

The NBA is already building a list of African players. Star NBA players from Africa include Dikembe Mutombo from the Democratic Republic of the Congo and Sudan's Manute Bol. Another player from Sudan, Luol Deng, played as an All-Star in the 2011–12 season, and Luc Mbah A Moute from Cameroon is a fan favorite. Masai Ujiri, general manager of the NBA's Toronto Raptors, is from Nigeria.

Ujiri has said that Africa offers a huge talent pool to the NBA. "Some tribes in Sudan and Senegal have an average height of six-foot-six," he said, "which also happens to be the size of the average NBA player. People in Nigeria, Mali, and Congo tend to be very big and physical. We need to build a strategy to go into these regions and cultivate the talent."

Make Connections

Basketball without Borders is the NBA and FIBA's global outreach program that unites young basketball players. Just as Naismith did when he started the sport, the organization believes that basketball can be used to bring about positive change in the areas of education, health, and wellness. The program picks top players who are nineteen and under from Africa, Asia, Europe, and Latin America. NBA players and coaches teach the young men basketball skills, as well as leadership, character development, and health. To promote friendship and acceptance between the groups, the young players are divided into teams without regard for nationality or race. Since the program began in 2001, 350 NBA players and coaches from thirty different teams have coached and taught more than 1,500 young people in eleven countries on five continents.

BASKETBALL IN ASIA

India

Basketball has been in India for a long time, ever since 1930. Indians loved the game because of its fast pace. By the twenty-first century, it was one of the most widely played sports in India, played at high schools and universities by both men and women. India has many championships for children and teenagers, as well as players at the college level. Unlike the American game, basketball in India does not follow seasons. Indian basketball has championships throughout the year for different age groups.

So far, India has produced many talented basketball players who have won fame in international basketball—but none who have been drafted by the NBA. Right now, though, the NBA is keeping an eye on a young Indian player named Satnam Singh Bhamara. By the time Satnam was fourteen, he was over seven feet tall and an amazing basketball player. Born in a small village to ordinary parents, Satnam won the attention of the NBA. He attended a Basketball without Borders camp—and then he won a scholarship to the IMG Academy, which trains athletes from around the world. Soon he was on the other side of the world from his village, training to be a basketball player in Florida. During every vacation, he went back home to play in basketball tournaments. The boy from the small town is now famous in India. They hope that in a few more years he will take their country to the NBA.

Japan

Basketball reached Japan early in the twentieth century through the YMCA. Japan's national league formed in 1917 and went on to win international championships. In the 1960s and 1970s, it was often a winner at the FIBA World Championship. Lately, though, it has fallen behind competition from China and the Middle East.

Japan continues to produce star players, though. One of these, Yuta Tabuse, was the first Japanese-born player in the NBA. Takuya Kawamura is another Japanese player who has joined the NBA.

Middle East

The Middle East region loves basketball. Oil-rich sheiks often sponsor the teams, offering salaries and **perks** that attract some of the world's best players. Countries like Lebanon, Iran, and Bahrain have teams that excel at FIBA's World Championships.

The game also works in the war-torn region to bring much-needed cooperation between groups that are usually in conflict. PeacePlayers, for example, is a Middle East charity that unites and educates both Jewish and Arab young people through basketball. The kids learn how to play basketball—and how to get along, despite their differences.

American players are also deciding to play for Middle East teams. When they do, they help break down some of the walls between Americans and this region of the world. "Basketball is universal," said one American player, Andre Pitts, who plays for an Iranian team, "so there's no color, no race; we just bond." Another American player for Iran, Garth Joseph, adds, "We have different cultures, different religions, so if we respect that we will get along very fine."

China

YMCA missionaries brought basketball to China shortly after the game was born. For years, the Chinese did not think of basketball as an American sport. Instead, it was *their* sport, the only Chinese sport that brought together people of all backgrounds to excite the entire nation.

In the 1930s, when the Communist party was rising to power in China, Communist soldiers played basketball to lift their spirits and create a feeling of **solidarity**. The Communist party loved the sport because it helped to bring people together, and the party continued to support the sport after it came to power in 1949. Chairman Mao himself, the leader of Communist China, loved basketball. He hated everything else about the West, from music to literature, but he totally approved of basketball.

With so many other forms of entertainment denied them once the Communists were in power, Chinese children and teenagers set up boards and hoops in alleys and courtyards. Meanwhile, the People's Liberation Army (the Chinese Communist party's military

Basketball has even played a role in international politics! Here, Chinese Vice Premier Wang Qishan holds an autographed basketball that President Obama gave him when they met in 2009 to discuss U.S.-China relations. Looking on is Chinese State Councilor Dai Bingguo.

branch) encouraged its more than 2 million members to play basketball because it built *camaraderie* and teamwork. With slogans like "Friendship First, Competition Second," basketball became the most popular way to have fun in China's military camps. Star players even received higher military ranks, along with perks such as separate dining rooms, cars, and expensive clothes. The country's best players were all from the military teams. One of these players, Wang Zhizhi, was China's first player to enter the NBA.

In modern-day China, where many young people have no brothers or sisters due to China's one-child policy, basketball offers a chance for kids to form connections with other kids. Basketball teams are like family.

Basketball was already popular before the NBA arrived there in 1987, when the games were first broadcast to Chinese television viewers. Now, however, it has become a craze. Across China, about 450 million people watch NBA games. Basketball superstars like Kobe Bryant, Kevin Garnett, and Lebron James have become household names. In 2002, when Yao Ming signed with the Houston Rockets, the Chinese were proud and thrilled. Their favorite sport was in the big time.

BASKETBALL IN EUROPE

As basketball spread into Asia, Africa, and the Americas, the game was also continuing to grow in Europe, mostly under the direction of FIBA.

EuroBasket is the main basketball competition of the men's national teams. The championship was first held in 1935. It is held every two years, but starting in 2017, it will change to a four-year cycle. Twenty-four teams take part in the final competition. Historically, the Soviet Union (which is now Russia) was the most successful nation, winning fourteen titles. Spain won the championship in 2009 and 2011, but had to give it up to France in 2013. EuroBasket has also served as the means by which European teams qualified for the FIBA Basketball World Cup and the Olympic teams.

The Euroleague, however, is the most important professional club basketball competition in Europe. FIBA members from as many as eighteen different countries compete in it. During the season, the Euroleague is broadcast on television in 199 countries, including the United States and Canada. In China, about 245 million households watch the Euroleague games weekly.

Make Connections

Sneaker companies are a group that has benefited from basketball becoming an international sport. Children, teenagers, and athletes around the world want to wear the same brand shoes that their basketball heroes wear.

While professional basketball is being played across Europe, the NBA is also drafting star European players. These include Tony Parker from France, who played for the San Antonio Spurs in 2014; Dirk Nowitzki from Germany (Dallas Mavericks); Marc Gasol from Spain (Memphis Grizzlies); and Goran Dragic from Slovenia (Phoenix Suns).

GLOBALIZATION AND BASKETBALL

Globalization is a word people talk about a lot in the twenty-first century. Sometimes they think it's a good thing, sometimes they worry that it could be a bad thing. Either way, it's a reality.

Globalization means that, more and more, we live in a world where we are citizens of Planet Earth as much as we are citizens of our separate countries. It's something that affects our lives at many levels. At the *economic* level, countries trade with each other; they build businesses in other countries; and they invest in businesses around the world.

All this means that one nation's economy can't be pulled out separately from all the rest: whatever helps or hurts one will end up affecting all the others as well. Culturally, we also share ideas and viewpoints around the world. People not only move from country to country more than they once did, but we also communicate far more easily today. The Internet has been a powerful tool for globalization.

And so has professional basketball. The NBA has brought a piece of American culture to countries around the globe, while at the same time, those countries are sending their players to the NBA. Basketball is crossing borders. It's linking people together in a global community that has one big thing in common: they all love basketball and its superstar players.

Words to Understand

agility: The ability to move quickly and easily.
inducted: Formally let someone into an organization.
endorse: Publicly show support for something.

BASKETBALL'S INTERNATIONAL SUPERSTARS

By 2014, there were nearly a hundred foreign-born players in the NBA. They came from forty different countries. NBA teams also played games in the Philippines, Brazil, England, and Spain, while at the same time, its American games were televised around the world to 750 million households in 212 countries.

The NBA today is a global force. And it's the players that help make it that way.

YAO MING

Yao Ming was born in Shanghai, China, in 1980. As a teenager, he played for the Shanghai Sharks. At seven-feet-six inches, he was a born basketball player who soon drew the notice of the NBA. He played for China in the 2000 Olympics, and then, in 2002, the Houston Rockets drafted him as their first overall pick.

Yao was truly a superstar. He was selected to start for the Western Conference in the NBA All-Star Game eight times, and he was named to the All-NBA Team five times. He reached the NBA Playoffs four times. Thanks to his help, the Rockets won a first-round

Yao Ming plays for the Houston Rockets against the Orlando Magic in a 2006 game.

series in the 2009 postseason, their first playoff series victory since 1997. He also continued to play for China in the FIBA Asian Championships, as well as at the 2004 Olympics.

Unfortunately, a series of foot and ankle injuries forced Yao to miss 250 games between 2005 and 2011. Yao decided he had had enough. In July 2011, he announced his retirement from professional basketball. In his eight seasons with the Rockets, Yao ranks sixth in total points and total rebounds, and second in total blocks.

HAKEEM OLAJUWON

Hakeem Olajuwon from Nigeria is one of the greatest players in NBA history. Until he was fifteen, he had only played soccer, never basketball. Olajuwon says, though, that playing soccer is what made him an amazing basketball player. It helped him to develop the *agility* and footwork for which he became famous.

After high school, Olajuwon moved from Nigeria to the United States. There he enrolled at the University of Houston, where he immediately got on the basketball team—and from there, he launched an NBA career, playing for the Rockets and the Raptors. When he retired in 2002, he was the ninth-leading scorer in league history. He has received the lasting honor of being *inducted* into the Basketball Hall of Fame.

Hakeem Olujuwan signs autographs during his time playing for the University of Houston.

Dirk Nowitzki shoots for the Dallas Mavericks in a game against the Detroit Pistons during the 2006–2007 season.

Patrick Ewing's college jersey sits in the Basketball Hall of Fame.

DIRK NOWITZKI

Dirk Nowitzki grew up in Germany. He didn't start playing basketball seriously until he was fifteen years old. His parents were both athletes, though (his mother played basketball and his father handball), and he inherited their abilities. In 1998, when he was eighteen, he was named "German Basketballer of the Year." From there, he headed to the NBA, where he played for the Mavericks. By 2014, he had scored 25,000 points.

PATRICK EWING

Many people forget that Patrick Ewing is an international player. He was born in Jamaica and didn't move to the United States until he was twelve years old. He played basketball in high school, and then won a basketball scholarship to Georgetown University. In the

Dikembe Mutombo uses his fame to do good back in Africa. Here he is explaining to Senegalese villagers how mosquito nets can stop the spread of malaria.

1895 NBA draft, he was the number-one pick, and he was the Rookie of the Year in 1986. His career just kept getting better, and he went on to be one of the biggest basketball stars of the 1990s. Before he retired in 2002, he played for the Knicks, the SuperSonics, and Magic. He has been inducted into the Basketball Hall of Fame.

DIKEMBE MUTOMBO

When Dikembe Mutombo left the Democratic Republic of Congo with an International Development scholarship to study at Georgetown University, he was hoping to become a doctor. Instead, the NBA took one look at the seven-foot-two player on the basketball court and knew that he had a great career ahead of him.

Mutombo started out by averaging 16.6 points per game as a rookie. Over the next ten years of his career, he averaged 12.4 points, 12.4 rebounds, and 3.5 blocks per game. An eight-time All-Star player, Mutombo is also one of the only two players to win Defensive Player of the Year four times. After playing for the Nuggets, Hawks, 76ers, Nets, Knicks, and the Rockets, Mutombo retired in 2009.

DIFFERENT BUT STILL THE SAME

Basketball has come a long, long way since James Naismith nailed those peach baskets to the wall. Naismith would probably have a hard time believing that his game has turned into an international sport, with celebrity players who make as much as $30 million a year (and that's not counting the money that companies like Nike, Adidas, and Reebok pay players to *endorse* their products).

Naismith, however, intended his game to be one that could grow and change; he wanted it to be a game that had room in it for all kinds of players with all kinds of skills. Today, more than ever, Naismith's goals are being realized.

Research Project

This chapter mentions that companies like Nike, Adidas, and Reebok pay basketball players to endorse their products. Find out more about endorsements, using the Internet, newspapers, and magazine articles. When did this practice get started? How much money do these companies pay players? Which players have received the most money for endorsements? Tell your class what you learn.

One other thing hasn't changed since Naismith's day. Despite all the fame and fortune, basketball continues to be a force that pulls people together. As we watch an exciting game between our favorite teams, we see past our differences. We're united with people all around the world who are watching that same game.

The players—whether they're professionals or a group of kids playing a pick-up game—know firsthand that basketball is all about pulling people together. Larry Brown, a college basketball coach, says, "All the successful teams I've ever seen have three characteristics: They play unselfish, they play together, and they play hard. . . . Basketball, more than any sport, is a team game."

Series Glossary of Key Terms

All-star games: A game where the best players in the league form two teams and play each other.

Assist: A pass that leads to scoring points. The player who passes the ball before the other scores a basket gets the assist.

Center: A player, normally the tallest on the team, who tries to score close to the basket and defend against the other team's offense using his size.

Championship: A set of games between the two top teams in the NBA to see who is the best.

Court: The wooden or concrete surface where basketball is played. In the NBA, courts are 94 feet by 50 feet.

Defensive: Working to keep the other team from scoring points.

Draft (noun): The way NBA teams pick players from college or high school teams.

Foul: A move against another player that is against the rules, mostly involving a player touching another in a way that is not fair play.

Jump shot: A shot made from far from the basket (rather than under the basket) while the player is in the air.

Offensive: Working to score points against the other team.

Playoffs: Games at the end of the NBA season between the top teams in the league, ending in the finals, in which the two top teams play each other.

Point guard: The player leading the team's offense, scoring points and setting up other players to score.

Power forward: A player who can both get in close to the basket and shoot from further away. On defense, power forwards defend against both close and far shots.

Rebound: Getting the ball back after a missed shot.

Rookie: A player in his first year in the NBA.

Scouts: People who search for new basketball players in high school or college who might one day play in the NBA.

Shooting guard: A player whose job is to take shots from far away from the basket. The shooting guard is usually the team's best long-range shooter.

Small forwards: Players whose main job is to score points close to the basket, working with the other players on the team's offense.

Steal: Take the ball from a player on the other team.

Tournament: A series of games between different teams in which the winning teams move on to play other winning teams and losing teams drop out of the competition.

Find Out More

ONLINE

African American Basketball History
www.tiki-toki.com/timeline/entry/28715/African-American-Basketball-History

Basketball and Globalization
www.newyorker.com/online/blogs/currency/2013/10/basketball-and-globalization.html

FIBA
www.fiba.com

James Naismith
www.kansasheritage.org/people/naismith.html

Olympic Basketball
www.insidehoops.com/olympics.shtml

IN BOOKS

Caponi-Tabery, Gena. *Jump for Joy: Jazz, Basketball, and Black Culture in 1930s America*. Boston: University of Massachusetts Press, 2008.

Coy, John. *Around the World*. New York: Lee & Low, 2005.

Gandolfi, Giorgi. *The Complete Book of Offensive Basketball Drills: Game-Changing Drills from Around the World*. New York: McGraw-Hill, 2009.

McCallum, Jack. *Dream Team: How Michael, Magic, Larry, Charles, and the Greatest Team of All Time Conquered the World and Changed the Game of Basketball Forever*. New York: Ballantine, 2013.

Rains, Rob. *James Naismith: The Man Who Invented Basketball*. Philadelphia, Penn.: Temple University Press, 2009.

Index

About the Author

Z.B. Hill is an author and publicist living in Binghamton, New York. He has written books on a variety of topics including mental health, music, and fitness.

Picture Credits